PREM'S ADVENTURES

BOOK FOUR

...in the Temple

Author Linda Look
Illustrator Crystal McLaughlin

Fables from around the world
for children and adults

Copyright © 2016 by Linda Look.

All rights reserved. No part of this book may be used or reproduced by any means, graphic, electronic, or mechanical, including photocopying, recording, taping or by any information storage retrieval system without the written permission of the author except in the case of brief quotations embodied in critical articles and reviews.

Balboa Press books may be ordered through booksellers or by contacting:

Balboa Press
A Division of Hay House
1663 Liberty Drive
Bloomington, IN 47403
www.balboapress.com
1 (877) 407-4847

Because of the dynamic nature of the Internet, any web addresses or links contained in this book may have changed since publication and may no longer be valid. The views expressed in this work are solely those of the author and do not necessarily reflect the views of the publisher, and the publisher hereby disclaims any responsibility for them.

ISBN: 978-1-5043-4428-9 (sc)
ISBN: 978-1-5043-4429-6 (e)

Library of Congress Control Number: 2015918537

Print information available on the last page.

Balboa Press rev. date: 0719/2016

CONTENTS

What a Three-Year-Old Knows

The Professor and the Tea

Fighting with Clouds

The Student in the Kitchen

The Gift of Insults

Sweet Tooth

The Thief Who Became Aware

The Gates of Paradise

The Examination

No Mistakes

The Author

Linda Look, a long-time fan of fable literature, is retired from a career in public policy research in Washington, DC. Now living in Wilmington, NC, she is also the developer of the Cosmic Karma Game.

The Illustrator

Crystal McLaughlin, a working artist specializing in illustration and graphic art, provided concept and final illustrations and the cover art. A resident of Myrtle Beach, SC, Crystal is also the illustrator of the Cosmic Karma Game.

General Support

Supporting development was provided by Elance online publishing services. Michael Z. Roulngul of Mizoram, India, assisted in the development of the illustrations. Charles M. Tolosa of Davado City, Philippines, assisted in the organization of material.

PROLOGUE

Prem's Adventures is the tale of the summer journey of a 12-year-old boy, Prem, who lives in a village in Southeast Asia. Prem is on his way to a temple, where he will spend his summer studying and meditating.

Along the way, Prem falls into one enchanting fable after another. Join Prem in this book as he goes . . .

... in the temple

Prem left home several weeks ago on his journey to the temple, and finally he was almost there. He could already see the roof of the temple gleaming on the far hill.

His activities will be rising before the sun comes up, meditating with the other boys, doing chores, and receiving instruction. He started walking quickly in anticipation.

What a Three-Year-Old Knows

When Prem reached the temple, he saw the temple master standing at the door. In Prem's excitement, he blurted out the hardest question he could think of: "What is the most important thing to do?" he asked the master.

"Do no harm, do good, and maintain the clarity of your mind," the master answered.

"That's it?" Prem asked.

"You sound disappointed, young one," the master said.

"Well," Prem hesitated. Then he said, almost whispering, "Even a three-year-old knows that."

"Maybe a three-year-old knows it," the master said, laughing. "But it is very hard to put into practice, even for an old man like me."

PERSEVERANCE
YOUR PRACTICE LASTS A LIFETIME.

The Professor and the Tea

Later that afternoon, Prem watched with interest as a distinguished gentleman entered the temple. "That's a professor from the university," one of the students whispered to Prem. "He is here to learn from our master."

Prem watched as the master greeted the professor and invited him to tea. The professor sat down and began to tell the master about the courses he taught. The master listened politely, and slowly began to pour the tea.

The professor was delighted to have such a distinguished listener, and talked more and more. The master continued to listen and continued to pour the tea. Finally, the tea flowed over the rim of the professor's cup and spilled onto the table.

"Stop, stop! What are you doing?" the professor sputtered as he jumped away from the table. "Can't you see my cup is full?"

"Just as your cup cannot hold any more tea when it is full, I cannot give you any knowledge when your mind is full," said the master.

RECEPTIVITY
THE MIND MUST BE OPEN TO RECEIVE.

Fighting with Clouds

Prem sat in meditation every morning with the other students, but he couldn't seem to quiet his mind. He thought about his new surroundings; he thought about the warm tea he would have after meditation; he thought about how his legs hurt. He thought, and he thought, and he thought.

"How can I ever meditate?" Prem asked the master. "I have a very active mind."

"You have a mind," the master said. "Your mind doesn't have you."

"But what about all of the thoughts?" asked Prem.

"Let them be like clouds," said the master. "You can observe them, but let them float by without getting involved with them."

MEDITATION
YOU DON'T HAVE TO TACKLE EVERY THOUGHT.

The Student in the Kitchen

The kitchen in the monastery was strictly off-limits to the students. Yet one of the boys, Anil, had sneaked into the kitchen twice already. The third time, one of the students reported it to the master. But to the students' dismay, the master acted as if nothing had happened.

The fourth time Anil slipped into the kitchen, the students protested to the master. "If you don't expel Anil," they said, "we will all leave the monastery."

"Boys, boys," the master said as he calmed the group. "If you want to leave the monastery, it is your choice. But Anil needs my teaching more than any of you. I will not expel Anil."

The students left the classroom to discuss this among themselves. "We are all deserving of compassion," the oldest boy told the group. "Anil needs instruction just as we do."

When the students returned, they reported that they wanted to continue classes with Anil. Anil was overcome with emotion, and never slipped into the kitchen again.

INCLUSION
WE ARE ALL PART OF THE WHOLE.

The Gift of Insults

There was a very mean-spirited teenager who lived in the village near the temple. One day this bad boy and his band of bad friends came to the temple and insulted the master. The master listened but did not respond.

Somewhat disappointed, the students gathered around the master and questioned him. "How could you endure such indignity?" they wanted to know.

"If someone offers you a gift and you do not receive it," the master replied, "to whom does the gift belong?"

"To the one who brought it?" guessed one of the students.

"Exactly," said the master. "It is not necessary to accept everything that is given to you."

CHOICE
IT'S YOUR DECISION WHAT TO ACCEPT.

Sweet Tooth

The temple was famous, and people came from far and wide to consult its master. One day a troubled mother came with her son. She complained that her son had an uncontrollable sweet tooth. "Would you please tell my son to stop eating sweets?" she asked the master.

"Come back in one week," the master told her. After only three days the mother and her son returned. "We have traveled a long way," she said. "Can you please tell my son now so we might begin our trip home?"

"I'm sorry," said the master, "but you must wait four more days." At the end of the week the mother and her son again returned. Addressing the boy, the master said sternly, "Boy! I order you to stop eating sweets."

"Yes, sir," the son said, bowing. The mother thanked the master, and she and her son started their journey home.

"Why didn't you tell her that last week?" Prem, who had been listening from the other room, asked the master.

"Because last week I was still eating sweets myself," laughed the master.

INTEGRITY
MASTER YOURSELF FIRST.

The Thief Who Became Aware

There were always people coming to the temple who wanted to improve themselves. One day even a thief came.

"Do you think you can help me improve myself?" the thief asked the master. "I will do anything you say, but I must inform you that I have accepted my destiny as a thief. I will not try to change that."

"No problem," said the master. "My teachings are not about thievery. My teachings are about awareness. As far as I am concerned, you may do anything you like as long as you do it in a state of awareness."

The thief was so happy to hear this that he left the temple whistling and skipping. But after three weeks, he returned to the temple walking slowly and dejectedly.

"You are wise, indeed," the thief said to the master. "Last night I was able to gain entry into a rich man's house, but when I looked at his jewels and money, they had no value for me. I became aware that I was losing myself over stones and coins."

AWARENESS
WHEN ILLUSIONS FALL AWAY, BEHAVIOR CHANGES.

The Gates of Paradise

The students were sitting in the shade in the temple yard late one afternoon when a large, fierce man came through the temple gates. He charged right past them and into the temple.

"They say you are wise," the man said loudly to the master. "Let's see if you can tell me the difference between heaven and hell."

"I cannot teach you anything," said the master. "You are too stupid to learn."

"What?" shouted the man. He couldn't believe his ears. He became so enraged that the veins in his forehead nearly popped out of his head.

"And, you stink!" the master exclaimed. The man's body began shaking uncontrollably with rage. He lunged at the master, intending to kill him.

"What you are feeling now is hell," the master said calmly.

The enraged man stopped in his tracks. He was overwhelmed with respect and gratitude, realizing that the master had risked his life to teach him this lesson.

"And what you are feeling now is heaven," the master said.

HEAVEN AND HELL
THE WORLD IS IN YOUR MIND.

The Examination

The master had been teaching the students the art of concentration since they had arrived. Now, it was time for a test. He took all the boys outside and pointed to a mango that was high in the tree.

"When I give the signal," the master said, "you throw a stone and knock the mango from the branch."

"Tun," the master said to the first boy, "do you see the tree, myself, and your brothers here?"

"I see all that you mention," Tun said confidently. The master was displeased. "Step back," he told Tun.

The master called on other boys with the same question for each. All failed the test. Then it was Prem's turn. "Look at the target," the master instructed. "Do you see the tree, the mango, and me?"

"No, sir," said Prem loudly. "I see only the mango and nothing else."

"Excellent," exclaimed the master. "You have passed the exam."

CONCENTRATION
A FOCUSED MIND PRECEDES SUCCESS.

No Mistakes

When summer ended, Prem prepared to leave the temple. The master could sense that Prem had something on his mind.

"What is bothering you, little brother?" the master inquired.

"I have learned so much this summer," Prem said, "but how will I keep from making mistakes when I am on my own?"

"Well, with wisdom," the master told Prem, smiling as he spoke.

"But how will I gain wisdom?" Prem asked in bewilderment.

"With experience," the master answered solemnly.

"But how will I gain experience?" Prem asked, more confused than ever.

"Aha!" said the master, smiling once again. "By making mistakes."

WISDOM
EVERY STEP IS PART OF THE PATH.

moving on ...

As Prem headed back to his village, he thought about his journey. He had so many insights about how his attitude was affecting his life experience. And the best insight of all was that it was all his own choice.

The Stories in This Collection

The stories in this collection have been adapted from a range of sources. All have been edited to fit the limitations of space and modified to meet the storyline of a boy on a journey.

What a Three-Year-Old Knows is adapted from a koan in *The Cave of Poison Grass*, by Seikan Hasegawa. (Great Ocean Publishers, Arlington, VA 1975, p. 43) It is based on verse 183 of the *Dhammapada*: "To avoid evil, to cultivate good, to purify the mind—this is the teaching of the Buddhas."

The Professor and the Tea is adapted from an anecdote in *Chop Wood, Carry Water: A Guide to Finding Spiritual Fulfillment in Everyday Life*, by Rick Fields. (Jeremy P. Tarcher/Putnam, NY, NY 1984, p.17) It is attributed to Buddhist monk Tanzan (1819-1892) of Japan.

Fighting with Clouds is developed from the concept of meditation: allowing an observed phenomenon to pass without mental or emotional attachment to it.

The Student in the Kitchen is adapted from a Zen parable in *Stories of the Spirit, Stories of the Heart, Parables of the Spiritual Path from Around the World*, by Christina Feldman and Jack Kornfield. (Harper Collins Publishers, NY, NY, 1991, p. 228)

The Gift of Insults is modified from the fable of the same name in *Kindness, A Treasure of Buddhist Wisdom for Children and Parents*, by Sarah Conover. (Eastern Washington University Press, Cheny and Spokane, WA, 2001, p.47)

Sweet Tooth is adapted from a story told in *Sufi Talks: Teachings of an American Sufi Sheikh*, by Robert Frager, Ph.D. It is attributed to 13th century Turkish Sufi master Nasruddin. (Quest Books, The Theosophical Publishing House, Wheaton, IL, 2012, p.189)

The Thief Who Became Aware is developed from "The Mahasiddha Nagabodhi The Red-Horned Thief" (#76) in *Masters of Mahamurda, Songs and Histories of the Eighty-Four Buddhist Siddhas*, by Keith Dowman. (State University of New York Press, Albany, NY, 1985, p. 350)

The Gates of Paradise is adapted from the parable of the same name (#57) in *Zen Flesh, Zen Bones: A Collection of Zen and Pre-Zen Writings*, by Paul Reps and Nyogen Senzaki. (Tuttle Publishing, VT, 1957, p. 80) It is attributed to Zen master Hakuin (1686-1768).

The Examination is adapted from the fable of the same name told at http://www.journeytothetruth.com.

No Mistakes is developed from the adage, "Good judgment comes from experience; experience comes from bad judgment." That adage is attributed to 13th century Turkish Sufi master Nasruddin. The story is retold in *The Beggar and the Secret of Happiness*, by Joel Izzy. (Algonquin Books, 2003, pp. 206-7.)

Lightning Source UK Ltd.
Milton Keynes UK
UKOW07f1602081216
289503UK00003B/5/P